Shih Tzu

Charles and Linda George

Created by Q2AMedia
www.q2amedia.com
Editor Jeff O' Hare
Publishing Director Chester Fisher
Client Service Manager Santosh Vasudevan
Project Manager Kunal Mehrotra
Art Director Harleen Mehta
Designer Deepika Verma
Picture Researcher Nivisha Sinha

Library of Congress Cataloging-in-Publication Data
George, Charles, 1949-
Shih tzu / [Charles George, Linda George].
p. cm. — (Top dogs)
Includes index.
ISBN 0-531-24935-2/978-0-531-24935-2 (pbk.)
1. Shih tzu—Juvenile literature. I. George, Linda. II. Title.
SF429.S64G46 2010
636.76—dc22
2010035037

This edition published by Scholastic Inc.,

Printed and bound in Heshan, China
232753 10/10
10 9 8 7 6 5 4 3 2 1

Picture Credits
t= top, b= bottom, c= center, r= right, l= left

Cover Page: Jerry Shulman/Photolibrary

Title Page: Callalloo Canis/Fotolia

4-5: Kaiser,Henryk T/Index Stock/Corbis; 5: Volina/Shutterstock; 6-7: Anne Kitzman/Bigstock; 7: Jupiterimages/Photolibrary; 8: Geri Lavrov/Getty Images; 8-9: Doxa Digital Imaging/ Istockphoto; 10: Darren K. Fisher/Shutterstock; 10-11: Jerry Shulman/Photolibrary; 12-13: Callalloo Canis/Fotolia; 13: Wilson Valentin/Istockphoto; 14: Anne Kitzman/ Shutterstock; 15: Anne Kitzman/Bigstock; 16-17: Callalloo Canis/Fotolia; 18: Anne Kitzman/ Shutterstock; 19: Gareth Brown/Corbis; 20-21: Matt Antonino/Dreamstime; 21: Laszlo Lim/ Dreamstime; 22: Purestock/Photolibrary; 22-23: Jason Lugo/Istockphoto; 24-25: Geri Lavrov/ Getty Images; 26: Coloroftime/Istockphoto; 26-27: Lon Dean, Seal Beach, CA; 28-29: Jeanell Norvell/Istockphoto; 30-31: Mary Bloom/West Minster Kennel Club; 31: Henny Ray Abrams/AP Photo.

Contents

What are Shih Tzus?

The Shih Tzu (*sheet sue*) was first raised in Tibet. Tibet is now controlled by China. Shih Tzu means "lion dog." Shih Tzus were once called Lhasa Lion Dogs or Fo Dogs. Lhasa is the capital of Tibet.

Fast Fact

Shih Tzus were first brought to the U.S. in the 1930s and 1940s.

For centuries, people in Tibet gave Shih Tzus as gifts to the leaders of China. For many years, Shih Tzus were owned only by rich and powerful families. Today, they are in many U.S. homes.

Everyone Loves Shih Tzus!

Shih Tzus are very small. They are called **toy dogs**. They are sweet and lively. They love to play! They love people. They really like children. They are also tough little dogs that bark a lot!

Fast Fact

Shih Tzus seem to think they are bigger than they really are.

Fast Fact

Train your Shih Tzu to be around people and other pets. If you don't, it may growl and bite.

Shih Tzus are good lap dogs. They love to be petted and cuddled. Their favorite place to be is near someone they love. They can get under your feet. So be careful where you step.

Shih Tzus and Kids

Shih Tzus get along with older children. Small children shouldn't play with Shih Tzus without an adult around. Shih Tzus are very small when they are young. They can get hurt if they are handled too roughly.

Fast Fact

Most small dogs bark a lot. They have to be trained to know when it is okay to bark.

Be careful when petting or playing with your Shih Tzu. Think of your Shih Tzu as a baby. Handle it gently! Never tease or pet your puppy too roughly. Never throw toys or food at your dog.

Fast Fact

A Shih Tzu has large eyes.

Tiny Puppies

Shih Tzu puppies are very small. They weigh only 4 to 8 ounces (0.1-0.2 kg) at birth. That's about as heavy as a bar of soap.

Fast Fact

There are usually 4 to 5 Shih Tzu puppies in a **litter**.

Fast Fact

Your Shih Tzu puppy's mouth gets sore when it's **teething**. Give it something to chew on!

A mother Shih Tzu needs plenty of room to snuggle and feed her puppies. The puppies **nurse** for at least six weeks. Then, they can have puppy food.

Choosing a Shih Tzu Puppy

Before you choose a puppy, look at all the puppies in the litter. Choose one with bright eyes. A male has more energy than a female. Choose a puppy that likes you!

Fast Fact

Male Shih Tzus are easier to **housetrain** than females.

Shih Tzus are house dogs. They should not live outside. They need a lot of care. It's best if your mom or dad can be home most of the time. You will need help taking care of these dogs.

Taking Care of your Shih Tzu

Your Shih Tzu puppy should have a soft, dry place to sleep. Your puppy will love sleeping on your bed. But when it's tiny, it should have its own bed.

Fast Fact

You might roll over on your puppy while sleeping. You don't want to hurt your puppy.

Fast Fact

You can block off a small corner of your kitchen as a play area for your puppy.

A puppy needs to eat food made just for puppies. Treats are okay for training, but don't give it too many. You don't want your puppy to gain too much weight! It also needs clean, cool water to drink.

How Big do Shih Tzus Get?

Shih Tzus are small dogs, even when they are fully grown. Adult Shih Tzus stand between 8 and 11 inches (20.3-27.9 cm) tall. They weigh 9-16 pounds (4.1-7.3 kg).

Fast Fact

Pick up your Shih Tzu like a football. Put your hand under its stomach and chest.

Shih Tzus are **sturdy** little dogs. They are a little longer than they are tall. Their bushy tails curl up over their backs. Tie the hair on their heads into a topknot so they can see where they are going.

Fast Fact

Even though they are little, Shih Tzus like to play rough. They like to play tug-of-war!

Brushing Hair and Clipping Nails

You should **groom** and gently brush your Shih Tzu every day. Start when your dog is still a puppy. Give your Shih Tzu a bath once a week. This keeps its **coat** clean and shiny.

Fast Fact

Shih Tzus don't like getting wet. Bathe them gently.

You can take your Shih Tzu to a groomer for a haircut. This makes it easier to take care of its coat. Its nails should be trimmed once in a while, too.

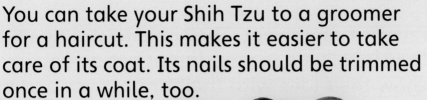

Fast Fact

A groomer can bathe your dog and trim its nails.

Sweet Shih Tzus

Shih Tzus are very sweet. They love to cuddle with you. They love lying in your lap or beside you. They show their love with their bright eyes and by barking. They also like to bounce, twirl, and lick you.

Fast Fact

Shih Tzus love to lick! They will lick your face as long as you let them.

Shih Tzus are good pets for people with **allergies**. These dogs have long hair, but they don't **shed** very much! Daily brushing removes any hair that needs to be shed.

Fast Fact

Some Shih Tzu owners put pretty bows in their dog's hair. Some dress them up in puppy clothes.

Shih Tzus Don't Need Much Room

Shih Tzus don't need a lot of room. They are happy in a very small home. They will nap on the couch or in a chair. They would rather curl up in your lap!

Fast Fact

If you want to play, your Shih Tzu will play. If you don't, it will rest beside you.

All dogs need exercise to stay healthy. Shih Tzus like to go outside every day for a walk. If you can't take your dog outside, let it play, run, and romp in the house.

Fast Fact

Shih Tzus have very short legs. Four blocks is far enough for them to get a healthy walk.

Loyal Friends

Shih Tzus love being house dogs! They are very **loyal** to their people. They are smart dogs. They love going for walks outside. They sniff where other animals have been. They like to explore and see new places.

Fast Fact

Shih Tzus are friendly to everyone they meet.

Always keep your Shih Tzu on its **leash** and **harness** when you take it for a walk. It's very curious. It may wander off and get lost! Mom or Dad should go with you when you walk your Shih Tzu.

Fast Fact

A Shih Tzu will try to save you from anything it thinks is dangerous. It will bark at big dogs.

Curious about Everything!

Shih Tzus bark at anything new. They bark when someone knocks on the door. They bark at people they don't know. Shih Tzus bark when they play. They also bark at animals and at strange noises.

Fast Fact

Shih Tzus bark when they are happy! If you have been gone for a while, they will bark "Hello!" when you get home!

A Shih Tzu makes a good watchdog. Let it know that new people and animals are okay. If you have other pets, it may take a while before they get along with your new puppy.

Fast Fact

When you come home, your Shih Tzu will sniff all over your body. It wants to know where you've been!

Shih Tzus Helping People

Shih Tzus were once herding dogs. Now, they are friendly pets. They can also be good **therapy dogs**. They like to visit people who are sick and who live alone.

A Shih Tzu is a good **companion**. A person who is home most of the time may like caring for a Shih Tzu. With a Shih Tzu there, a person won't feel so lonely!

Best of the Breed

Owners of Shih Tzus sometimes enter them into **dog shows**. The Westminster Kennel Club holds a show every year. In 2010, a Shih Tzu named Austin Powers won Best of Breed. This means he was the best Shih Tzu in the show. The Westminster dog show takes place in New York City.

Fast Fact

This Shih Tzu's full name is Ch. Hallmark Jolei Austin Powers. He lives near Toledo, Ohio.

In the first 4 months of 2010, Austin Powers won Best in Show at 8 different dog shows. Best in Show means that the show judge thought Austin Powers was the best dog in the entire show—not just the best Shih Tzu!

Fast Fact

Two other champion Shih Tzus from the same **kennel** were named Jezebel and Raggedy Andy.

Glossary

Allergy – a medical condition in which a person sneezes or otherwise reacts to something in the air

Coat – hair

Companion – friend

Cross – when one breed of dog is mated with a different breed, the puppy is called a "cross"

Dog show – a contest where dog breeders bring their dogs, and judges decide which dog best represents that breed

Groom – comb and brush an animal's hair

Harness – a web of straps that go around a dog's chest and neck

Housetrain – teach a pet to go to the bathroom in a specific place in the house

Kennel – a place where dogs are raised and trained

Leash – a strap that attaches to a harness to help control a dog when it's being taken for a walk

Litter – a group of puppies born to a mother dog at the same time

Loyal – faithful

Mixed breed – a dog (or other animal) whose parents aren't of the same breed; a cross between two or more breeds

Newborn – a dog (or other animal) that was just born

Nurse – drink milk from a mother's breast

Pure-bred – a dog (or other animal) whose parents were both of the same breed

Shed – lose hair

Sturdy – strong

Teething – when teeth grow in

Therapy dog – a dog trained to visit people who are sick or who live alone

Top knot – a bunch of hair on top of a dog's head, usually tied with a bow

Toy dog – a certain class of very small dogs

Index